Manikarnika: The Queen Of Jhansi

By

Olive R. Hanes

Table of contents

Introduction

Reading about a woman who heroically and alone fought for her kingdom, self-respect, family, and the people of her realm stands out in a world full of manufactured rulers, characters, and other personalities. Her nickname was Manu, and she was born into a Marathi brahmin family. Her parents were Maharashtrian natives who were related to Nana Sahib; it is believed that they were both first cousins. In the court of the Bithoor region of the Peshwa of Bithoor, her father, Moro Pant Tambe, vaulted. Manikarnika was raised by an honest guy who called her chabeli, which is Hindi for "playful," because of her joyful, playful, and well-known nature.

An important part of the 1857 uprising was played by Rani Lakshmibai of Jhansi. She heroically fought alongside the British force. She took issue with the British law that prevented her adoptive son from becoming the monarch. She was one of the major drivers driving the anti-British uprising. She exhibited unmatched courage, which is uncommon.

Early Life

Rani Lakshmibai was born on November 19, 1828, in Varanasi, India, into a Marathi Karhade Brahmin family (some sources state 1835). She went by the name Manikarnika Tambe and went by the nickname Manu. Her mother was Bhagirathi Sapre, and her father was Moropant Tambe (Bhagirathi Bai). Her parents are from the Maharashtrian village of Tambe in the Guhagar Taluka in the Ratnagiri district. When she was four years old, her mother passed away. Her father was the Kalyan Pranth war commander. Her father served Peshwa Baji Rao II of the district of Bithoor. She was given the Peshwa's nickname "Chhabili," which translates to "beautiful" and "lively and cheery."

It was difficult for girls to obtain an education at that time because schools only allowed male participants, so education for girls was only provided at home, and even then, only for a select few girls. However, Lakshmibai's parents supported her education, so she was able to attend school. Manu was a very intelligent and diligent student who was eager to learn everything. Because of this, she combined her studies with childhood friends Nana Sahib and Tatya Tope's Mala Khamba, shooting, horsemanship, fencing, and other sports. Many of the patriarchal cultural expectations for women in Indian society at the time were contrasted by Rani Lakshmibai. She was also renowned for her original opinions and her boldness in defying social conventions in front of the entire society.

Between the palace and the temple, Rani Lakshmibai was used to traveling on horseback with escorts, though occasionally she was carried in a palanquin. Sarangi, Pavan, and Baadal were some of her horses. According to historians, when she fled the fort in 1858, she was riding Baadal. Currently, the Rani Mahal, her residence, serves as a museum. It houses a collection of artifacts dating from the 9th to the 12th century AD.

History of Jhansi,1842 May 1857

Even Manikarnika's personal life took numerous twists and turns. At the age of 14, Manikarnika was married to the Maharaja of Jhansi, Gangadhar Rao Newalkar, in May 1842 and was afterward dubbed Lakshmibai (or Laxmibai) in honor of the Hindu goddess Devi Lakshmi and according to the Maharashtrian tradition of women being given up a new name after marriage. She gave birth to a child in September 1851 who was later given the name Damodar Rao but who passed away four months later from a severe illness. The day before he passed away, the Maharaja adopted Anand Rao, the cousin of Gangadhar Rao, who was given the new name Damodar Rao. A British political officer who was present for the adoption was given a letter from the Maharaja instructing that the child be treated with dignity and that his widow be given control of Jhansi for the rest of her life.

Before breakfast, Rani would engage in weightlifting, wrestling, and steeplechasing. She was a smart, understatedly dressed woman who controlled with a professional demeanor.

The British East India Company, led by Governor-General Lord Dalhousie, applied the Doctrine of Lapse following the death of the Maharaja in November 1853, rejecting Damodar Rao's claim to the throne and annexing the state to its territories. This was done because Damodar Rao (born Anand Rao) was an adopted son. She yelled out, "Main apni Jhansi nahi doongi," after learning this (I shall not surrender my Jhansi). Rani Lakshmibai was awarded a pension of Rs. 60,000 per year in March 1854 and was told to leave the palace and the fort. After the passing of her husband, Rani Lakshmibai of Jhansi wished for the East India Company to recognize her adopted son as the rightful heir to the throne. The British rejected this demand. According to the Doctrine of Lapse, any princely state or territory that belonged to the British East India Company would be automatically annexed if the ruler passed away without a male heir. Lord Dalhousie is said to have used this policy. The British refused to accept Raja Gangadhar Rao, the monarch of Jhansi, as his heir when he passed away without a natural son. This did not sit well with Rani Lakshmibai, and she vowed to keep Jhansi hers at all costs, saying, "I shall not give my Jhansi" (Main meri Jhansi nahi doongi).

Rule and Revolt of Lakshmi Bai

The 22-year-old refused to give the British control over Jhansi. Lakshmi Bai was proclaimed monarch of Jhansi and afterward changed her name to Jhansi ki Rani Lakshmi Bai shortly after the 1857 revolt, which broke out in Meerut, began. She made decisions on behalf of a young heir. She promptly gathered her forces and assumed command of the rebels in the bundelkhand region, leading the British uprising. Nearby mutineers traveled to Jhansi to lend their support.

The Indian Rebellion began at Meerut on May 10th, 1857. The British political officer Captain Alexander Skene granted Rani's request to create a body of armed men for her protection after hearing about the revolt in Jhansi. During the widespread upheaval in the summer of 1857, the city was comparatively tranquil, but the Rani held a pompous Haldi Kumkum ceremony in front of all the women of Jhansi to reassure her subjects and persuade them that the British were cowards and that they should not be scared of them.
Lakshmi Bai had been hesitant to revolt against the British up to this time. The 12th Bengal Native Infantry rebels took control of the Star Fort of Jhansi, which housed the treasure and magazine, in June 1857. After promising the British they would do them no harm in exchange for their surrender, the rebels broke their word and massacred 40 to 60 European officers of the garrison, along with their

wives and children. Rani's role in this atrocity is still up for discussion. She was referred to as the "Jezebel of India" and "the young rani upon whose head rested the blood of the slain" in a post-rebellion letter by an army doctor, Thomas Lowe.

After extorting a sizable quantity of money from the Rani and making threats to blow up the palace where she resided, the troops left Jhansi four days after the killing. After that, the Rani felt compelled to assume control of the city as the only source of authority there and wrote to Major Erskine, commissioner of the Saugor division, outlining the circumstances that had prompted her to do so. Erskine wrote back on July 2 asking her to "handle the District for the British Government" until a British Superintendent showed up. The mutineers' attempt to usurp the crown of rival prince Sadashiv Rao (the nephew of Maharaja Gangadhar Rao), who had been caught and imprisoned, was stopped by Rani's men.

The soldiers of Company allies Orchha and Datia then invaded Jhansi to divide the city between themselves. The Rani requested assistance from the British but received no response because the governor-general now felt that she was guilty of the massacre. She organized warriors, including some from former feudatories of Jhansi and parts of the mutineers, which were able to defeat the invaders in

August 1857, and set up a foundry to make guns to be used on the fort's walls. She still intended to hold Jhansi for the British at this point.

Siege of Jhansi

Jhansi enjoyed tranquility under Rani's administration from August 1857 until January 1858. Even though the British had promised to send troops to keep control, a group of her advisers who sought independence from British rule gained more ground as a result of their failure to do so. The fort had large guns that could shoot over the town and the surrounding area when the British soldiers eventually arrived in March, and they discovered it to be well-defended. Hugh Rose, the commander of the British forces, allegedly requested the city's surrender, threatening to destroy it if it was refused. According to the same source, the Rani declared the following after careful consideration: "For independence, we struggle. According to Lord Krishna, if we win the battle, we will reap the rewards of our success, but if we lose and are murdered, we will unquestionably gain salvation and eternal glory." For instance, no reference to a surrender demand can be found in other sources. On March 23, 1858, when Sir Hugh Rose invaded Jhansi, she defended the city from British forces.

Jhansi was bombarded beginning on March 24 but was heavily retaliated upon, and the defenses were restored. When they battled the British on March 31, an army of more than 20,000 soldiers led by Tatya Tope was deployed to liberate Jhansi, but they were unable to do so. A portion of the British soldiers continued the siege while engaged in combat with Tatya Tope's forces, and on April 2 it was decided to attack through a wall breach. At various points, four columns attacked the defenses, and anyone trying to scale the walls were heavily fired upon. Two other columns had already arrived in the city and were moving in tandem toward the palace. Every street and apartment of the palace experienced stubborn resistance. No mercy was shown to anyone, including women and children, during the street combat that went on into the following day. According to Thomas Lowe, "No sorrowful mercy was to mark the collapse of the city." Rani left the palace and went to the fort, where she sought advice before deciding that since she couldn't win the city by fighting, she should depart and either join Tatya Tope or Rao Sahib (Nana Sahib's nephew).

Sensing that only war would do, the tenacious organized army and trained women in combat. Rani Laxmi Bai led the attack when the British army arrived in Jhansi while carrying her son Damodar

Rao on her back. The queen refused to submit and, while traveling to the Kalpi fortress, murdered some enemy soldiers while holding two swords in each hand.

Tradition has it that she jumped upon her horse, Badal, from the fort while carrying Damodar Rao on her back; they both survived, but the animal perished. With her son by her side, the Rani fled throughout the night while being guarded. The warriors Khuda Bakhsh Basharat Ali, who served as the escort's commanding officer, Gulam Gaus Khan, Dost Khan, Lala Bhau Bakshi, Moti Bai, Sunder-Munder, Kashi Bai, Deewan Raghunath Singh, and Deewan Jawahar Singh were all present. [Reference needed] With a handful of her guards, she fled to Kalpi where she joined other rebel forces, including Tatya Tope. They took control of Kalpi and got ready to defend it. British troops, led by Rani herself, invaded Kalpi on May 22 but were once more routed.

Betrayal

While under Company Rule (the East India Company), Jhansi had preserved its independence from British India, and the Maharaja continued to support the British Empire. They didn't refuse to acknowledge Rani and her adoptive son for any reason other than the outrageous mismanagement and avarice of the chairman of the East India Company.

But…

This is how they operate.

However, Rani Lakshmibai famously declared that she would not surrender her Jhansi to the British.

"Mera Jhansi nahi dengee!"

"मेरा झाँसी नहीं देंगी!"

However, Rani Lakshmibai was told to leave the palace and fort in March 1854 and given an annual pension of Rs. 60,000. A British politician at the time wrote of her that the reason they didn't hire her was not that they felt she lacked the necessary skills.

"a woman who is highly regarded and esteemed, and who I believe is more than capable of answering such a charge"

1988 British Massacre author Antonia Fraser's work in "Warrior Queens"
Lakshmibai asked the British for permission to assemble a defense force when word of the Indian Rebellion of 1857 reached Jhansi, and they agreed. The British were assured their safety when the rebels arrived in Jhansi if they laid down their guns and fled. However, this time it was the British men who were betrayed; 50 to 60 of them, along with their spouses and kids, were killed. Then they turned on Lakshmibai and demanded payment, threatening to blow up the palace unless she did.

After the killing, she seized charge of Jhansi and requested permission to "rule the District for the British Government" in a letter to the British. To defend her realms from both a rival claim to her husband's throne and from rebel forces seeking to seize Jhansi for themselves, she had to establish a foundry.
The British, who had by this point believed that she was responsible for the massacre, were unable to assist her in defeating them all. Peace reigned in Jhansi from August 1857 to January 1858, which

increased the locals' conviction that the city should and could be free of British domination.

Rani Rebels

Rani Lakshmibai continued to back the British, nonetheless. She had had enough, though, when the British troops, under the direction of commander Sir Hugh Rose, arrived and threatened to destroy Jhansi if they didn't submit. She announced,

"We struggle for freedom. According to Lord Krishna, if we win the battle and reap the rewards, yet lose and perish in the fray, we will undoubtedly gain redemption and eternal glory.

“हम स्वतंत्रता के लिए लड़ते हैं। भगवान कृष्ण के शब्दों में, यदि हम विजयी हैं, तो हम जीत के फल का आनंद लेंगे, यदि युद्ध के मैदान में पराजित और मारे गए, तो हम निश्चित रूप से अनन्त महिमा और मोक्ष अर्जित करेंगे। ”

In a city of 220,000 people, she organized a voluntary army of 14,000 men and recruited 15,000 sepoys or Indian troops who had previously served the British. Lakshmibai was unfortunately forced to abandon the palace for the fort and subsequently the fort for nearby Gwalior because of the fighting, and this moment has been immortalized in countless statues and paintings.

Fight to Gwalior

The leaders, including Rao Sahib, Tatya Tope, the Nawab of Banda, and the Rani of Jhansi, once more escaped. They arrived in Gwalior and joined the Indian army occupying the city at the time (Maharaja Scindia having fled to Agra from the battlefield at Morar). They continued to Gwalior to seize the vital Gwalior Fort, but the rebel soldiers entered the city unopposed. With Rao Sahib serving as his governor (subedar) in Gwalior, the rebels proclaimed Nana Sahib to be the Peshwa of a reborn Maratha kingdom. The Rani tried unsuccessfully to convince the other rebel commanders to be ready to defend Gwalior against an impending British onslaught. On June 16, General Rose's soldiers captured Morar before successfully attacking the city.

A troop of the 8th (King's Royal Irish) Hussars, commanded by Captain Heneage, engaged the sizable Indian force led by Rani Lakshmibai on June 17 in Kotah-ki-Serai, close to the Phool Bagh of Gwalior, as it attempted to flee the area. 5,000 Indian troops were killed by the 8th Hussars when they charged into the Indian force, including any Indian "above the age of 16". They grabbed two rifles and carried on the assault through the Phool Bagh camp. According to an eyewitness account of the battle, Rani Lakshmibai attacked one of the hussars while wearing a sowar's uniform. Despite Rani's small force size, she managed to win the battle, The British army was defeated thanks to the Sirdars' exceptional bravery and Rani's battle tactics and bravery. The Rani was responsible for the day's success. The British war trumpet sounded the following morning (18th) before dawn. Some soldiers were seduced by the Maharajah Jayaji Rao's pardon announcement and joined the British. Additionally, word came in that two brigades that were allied with Rao Saheb once more switched to the British.

The last day of the fight appears to be today, Rani Lakhsmi Bai commanded Ramachandra Rao Deshmukh. Consider taking care of my kid Damodar more important than taking care of yourself if I pass away. One more thing: in the event of my passing, please see to it that my body is not taken by anyone who does not follow my religion. Rose won that day, as was to be expected. A sizable portion of the revolutionary army was destroyed. The British ended up with their weaponry. Swift as a flood, the British force stormed inside the fort.

Rani had no choice but to leave that location, so she took it. The Rani rode off while gripping the horse's reins in her teeth and displaying her sword with both hands. Raghunatha Simha, Ramachandra Rao Deshmukh, and a few Pathan Sirdars were present. They were surrounded by the British army.

Blood was gushing everywhere. On the western horizon, the sun was the same color. Darkness was drawing near. A dagger was thrown at Rani's chest by a British soldier who was extremely close by. She felt it hit her slightly below the chest. A soldier was killed by the Rani. Her body was gushing blood. There was, however, no time for rest. She was being pursued by the British soldiers. A shot from the gun or a British soldier who arrived there struck Rani to the right as she prepared to cross the Swarnarekha Canal. Rani ended him by flashing the sword with her left hand.

Even the horse she selected at the dangerous hour was of no assistance. Its thigh was paralyzed. She was gushing blood from her stomach. A British soldier who followed her quickly cut her with a sword, tearing her right face. Her eyeball had been torn. Even then, she severed that soldier's arm with her left hand.

The Rani's bodyguard, Gul Mohamed, was unable to contain his grief. He started to sob as he did so, a brave fighter. They used cold water to cleanse the face. They filled her mouth with holy Ganga water. After a little period of recovery, she mumbled, "Hara Hara Mahadev," with shaking lips. She then fell into unconsciousness. The Rani was assisted by Raghunath Simha and Ramachandra Rao Deshmukh in getting off her horse. A little while later, Rani finally managed to open her eyes. She was mumbling verses from the Bhagavad Gita that she had memorized as a child. Her final words were, "Vasiudeva, I bow to you," as her voice grew weaker. Jhansi's fortune was determined. A few residents burned her body after she passed away.

After three days, the British had taken Gwalior. Hugh Rose wrote that Rani Lakshmibai is "personable, smart, and beautiful" and that she is "the most dangerous of all Indian leaders" in the British account of this conflict. In the words of

Rose, "I saw her bones and ashes under a tamarind tree under the Rock of Gwalior, where she was buried with much ceremony."

Her tomb is located in Gwalior's Phool Bagh neighborhood.

Descendant

The young prince was reportedly present at the battle of Gwalior with his mother's warriors and family, according to a narrative allegedly written by "Damodar Rao". He fled from Rao Sahib of Bithur's camp with other survivors (about 60 retainers, 60 camels, and 22 horses), and because the villagers of Bundelkhand dared not help them out of fear of retaliation from the British, they were left to live in the wilderness and endure severe hardships. About 12 survivors remained after two years, and they, along with another group of 24 people they came across, went in search of Jhalrapatan, where there were still more Jhansi refugees. The memoir of Damodar Rao of Jhansi, who gave himself over to a British official, finishes in May 1860. At that time, he was given a pension of Rs. 10,000, seven retainers, and was under Munshi Dharmanarayan's care. The entire memoir was published in Marathi in Itihasachi Aaa Saheli by Kelkar, Y. N. (1959). ("Voyages in History"). This text most likely represents a written version of the prince's life stories that were previously only known through oral tradition.

Cultural depictions and statues

Lakshmibai statues depicting her with her son bound to her back can be found throughout India. She is honored by having three institutions named after her: Maharani Laxmi Bai Medical College in Jhansi, the Lakshmibai National University of Physical Education in Gwalior, and Lakshmibai National College of Physical Education in Thiruvananthapuram. In 2013, Jhansi's Rani Lakshmi Bai Central Agricultural University was established. The Andaman and Nicobar Islands in the Bay of Bengal are home to the Rani Jhansi Marine National Park. The Rani of Jhansi Regiment was an Indian National Army women's division. Two postage stamps were released in 1957 to mark the rebellion's 100th anniversary. Indian literature, poetry, and film frequently glorify Rani Lakshmibai as a person who was fully committed to the cause of Indian independence straightforwardly.

The Indian Coast Guard vessel ICGS Lakshmi Bai was named after her.

Lakshmibai was named one of the "Top Ten Badass Wives" of all time by Time magazine in 2011...

बुंदेले हरबोलों के मुँह हमने सुनी कहानी थी, खूब लड़ी मर्दानी वह तो झाँसी वाली रानी थी।।

Translation: "We have heard this tale from the bards of Bundela: "She battled bravely like a warrior woman; she was the queen of Jhansi."

For Marathi speakers, there is a similarly well-known ballad about the brave queen that was written by B. R. Tambe, a poet laureate of Maharashtra and a member of her clan, at the location close to Gwalior where she died in battle. A few of the stanzas go like this:

रे हदिबांधवा, थांब या स्थळीं अश्रु दोन ढाळीं /

ती पराक्रमाची ज्योत मावळे इथे झाशिवाली / ... /

घोड्यावर खंद्या स्वार, हातात नंगि तिर्वार / खणखणा करति ती वार / गोर्यांची कोंडी फोडति पाडति वीर इथे आली /

मर्दानी झाशीवाली!

Translation: You, inhabitants of this region, stand here and weep a tear or two for this is the location where the brave lady of Jhansi was laid to rest after breaking the British siege while riding a strong steed and brandishing a naked sword.

Aftermath

She engaged in valiant and fierce combat while dressed as a guy. She urged the natives to bury or cremate her body because she did not want the British to find it. Her funeral is thought to have taken place the same day close to the location where she was murdered with the help of one of her maids. Following the surrender of Jhansi, the British hanged her father, Moropant Tambey. Damodar survived the war after his mother passed away and lived in abject poverty in the bush with his mentors. He was present at the battle of Gwalior with his mother's troops and family, according to a narrative that purports to be written by Damodar Rao. They were forced to live in the wilderness and endure numerous hardships when he fled Rao Sahib of Bithur's camp since the locals in Bundelkhand dared not help him for fear of retaliation from the British. A report claims that he took shelter in Jhalrapatan before meeting Raja Pratapsinh of Jhalrapatan with the assistance of some longtime confidants. One of Damodar Rao's guardians asked British political officer Flink for his forgiveness. After he submitted to the British, he was dispatched to Indore. Sir

Richard Shakespeare, the local political operative, had Munshi Dharmanarayan, a Kashmiri teacher, watch over him and instruct him in Marathi, English, and Urdu. Damodar received a yearly pension of 10,000 and was only permitted to retain seven followers (the rest were forced to leave).

He married and made Indore his home. After the passing of his first spouse, he remarried the Shivre family. He gave birth to a boy named Lakshman Rao in 1904. Later, after the Company's rule in India came to an end, he also petitioned the British Raj for recognition, but his request was denied. On May 28, 1906, Damodar Rao passed away. His son Lakshman Rao was left behind.

Damodar Rao never received an inheritance from the British, but the British Raj gave him a grant instead.
Because of her fortitude, bravery, and forward-thinking view on the empowerment of women in India in the 19th century, Rani LaxmiBai became well-known, and because of her sacrifices, she is loved by every Indian citizen. She was honored with bronze sculptures in Gwalior and Jhansi.

As a woman who can read the Bible and wield a sword with equal strength as a man, she represents true female empowerment even in current times.

She battled for numerous other causes in addition to defending her realm. She was able to set many examples for society by defending her adopted child's right to fight for freedom to live and rule rather than turn into Sati. As a result, she still rules in people's hearts and is remembered indelibly in the history of the National Movement.

In 1957, two postage stamps were released to commemorate the Queen's birthday.

Following the battle, Commander Sir Hugh Rose wrote about her, praising her for being "personable, smart, and lovely." A "kind of Indian Joan of Arc," she is "exceptional in her bravery, intellect, and perseverance" and is "the most dangerous of all Indian leaders."

Colonel Malleson noted twenty years after her passing, in 1878, that she was "ill-treated into rebellion" despite what the British said, and that she lived and died for her country.

The East Indian Company's incompetence and avarice led to this uprising, which ultimately resulted in the loss of its governmental authority and the establishment of Queen Victoria as Empress of India. Lakshmibai died in 1827; India did not become independent until 1947, a period of almost 90 years.

Conclusion

Numerous books, movies, works of art, and even video games have been inspired by her narrative. She is most usually represented as a warrior queen who rides into battle while carrying a child on her back. The flexibility that infant carriers offer is appealing to those of us who want to observe the fierceness of a mama bear in action; you can't do that with a stroller.

But is it an accurate portrayal of her? The child's age difference has already been mentioned, but what about her personality? Does this restrict her to a maternal trope? Although she could have been described as a mother by the men of her time, they praised her for being intelligent, strong, and professional—qualities that we now tend to associate with men. Many of the articles I read about her described her as a "tomboy."

Additionally, keep in mind that the child was only adopted because both Indians and British citizens believed a woman should not govern without a husband or son (even if they acknowledged that she was capable). There has to be a man involved for her to be legitimate. So if there hadn't been a baby, would you have noticed if she had been depicted riding into combat with a sword raised? Would it be as acceptable if she weren't shown as being a mother? Would this statue be so well-known if she had been fighting simply for her throne? Would it have been made at all?

These are some of the questions I discovered myself asking as I completed research on her.

Her progressive vision for the liberation of women in India in the 19th century, her acts of sacrifice, and her strength, courage, and intelligence made her a symbol of the Indian independence movement.

www.ingramcontent.com/pod-product-compliance
Lightning Source LLC
LaVergne TN
LVHW052114160826
845678LV00015B/3546

* 9 7 9 8 3 5 5 3 4 2 9 4 4 *